This work was originally written as a research paper for a graduate level Women's Studies Course.

All referenced Video Games are copyrighted by their original game developers, publishers.

References to copyrighted and research materials are posted in the "works Cited" section of the text.

INTRODUCTION

In the mid-1980s, my family got a Nintendo Entertainment System for Christmas. Although I think the present was really bought by my father for my younger brother, the NES quickly became a family present. My mother, brother, and myself all spent time playing various games on the console. Mom and Dad spent a large amount of time fishing in *The Black Bass* (1988). As a family we'd race on the Power Pad or shoot the laughing dog in *Duck Hunt* (1985).

The games that probably got the most play time in our house were *Super Mario Brothers* (1985) and *The Legend of Zelda* (1986). Both of these games feature a Male Hero who has to go through the game to rescue a Princess. It was just a thing: Princesses get captured and need heroes to rescue them. That's the way the world worked.

Even though my brother played far more often than I did, I never had the assumption that video games were 'boy toys.' I have clear memories of my mother mapping dungeons in *Zelda*, working to save the Princess from the evil Gannon.

I never noticed that it was always the princess that was

being rescued, until my brother began to play *Metroid* (1986). In the game *Metroid,* the player controls a character named Samus Aran, who travels throughout the game trying to rescue her home planet from Space Pirates and a master monster called "Mother Brain." It was only when my brother defeated Mother Brain and Samus removed her helmet that my brother, the player, learned that Samus was a girl.

Though my memory could be lying, I seem to remember my brother being annoyed by that revelation. He'd called the figure on screen "My guy" a lot. 'My guy keeps dying' and 'my guy has a cannon.' To suddenly find out that the 8-pixel 'guy' he'd been playing for days was a woman? He was annoyed. Or at least, that's what I remember.

This book sprung from a research paper I presented in 2011 to a Student Conference while working on my Master's Degree at the University of Houston, Clear-Lake. I was in a class and given the instruction to research "whatever woman studies topic I like" and decided that since Video Games play a large part of my life, I would look into this fascinating topic. At the time, my professor urged me to submit the paper to various scholarly journals. It was only recently, when I started working on my regular blogs for Land of the Nerds that I decided I needed to expand this, to make a more steady work out of it.

While gender should not matter in video game play and design, it does. Female game characters have transitioned from rescued princess to sex kitten to complex, three-dimensional characters that exist for more than traditional roles. Trans-gendered play and sexuality in games played within the home can be perceived as a threat by some players. Online, cross-gendered play is perceived to be a larger threat because of online interaction. Throughout this paper, I hope to investigate trends in female video game characters, discuss the options of gender and sexuality in two video game series, explain the evolution of Lara Croft, and discuss gender in online role-playing games.

A note on character types within video games. While I could reasonably assume that many of my readers are already familiar with the terms and terminology related to character types., there is a chance that some of you are not familiar with video game terminology, especially as it relates to the characters.

There are two different terms used to describe the character controlled by the player in video games. The first, player character or "PC" is a general term used to describe the playable character. The second term, "avatar" refers to a character played in an online, interactive environment, like a mass multiplayer online role-playing game (i.e. *World of Warcraft*).

For the purpose of my writing, I will use the term "PC" or "playable character" to refer to any character in a single-player or non-online video game environment. I will use the term "avatar" to describe characters played in multiplayer or online games. I will also use "PC" or playable character" to describe secondary characters within the game that are controlled by the video game players.

I will use the term "NPC" or "non-player character" to refer to characters controlled by the video game, as these are characters in the game that are *not* controlled by the players. NPCs can be antagonists, love interests, shopkeepers, any character that the player does not control within the world of the video game.

A note on Spoilers: This book will contain spoiler information on a wide variety of video games and movies, particularly when the spoilers can help enhance an understanding of characters and their roles in their games.

Author's note: I wrote this piece well before the Gamergate scandal, and I considered briefly adding a section in the text about the problem, but decided against it. Gamergate relates to developers and press, and my writing here focuses on video games, specifically those of the first decade of this century.

Thirty Characters

One of the best-known magazines for video game players is *Game Informer,* a monthly magazine published by *Game Stop,* one of the largest video game retailers in the United States. The magazine has been in circulation since 1991, and as of June, 2013, *Game Informer* was the third-most circulated magazine in the United States.

It is the job, the livelihood of the *Game Informer* writers and staff to stay abreast of the trends in video gaming. Home video game consoles have been in existence since the early 1970s, though grew in popularity with the Atari and home computers in the 1980s.

The first decade of this millennium saw an explosion of videogames as an art form. Video game console technology exploded. In 2000, the big new console was the Sony Playstation 2, followed shortly by the Nintendo Gamecube, and Microsoft's Xbox. 2005-2006 marked the release of a newer generation of consoles, the Sony Playstation 3, the Xbox 360, and the Nintendo Wii. At the time of this writing, each of the major game consoles have released their newest consoles: Playstation 4, Xbox One, and Nintendo Wii U.

With the explosion of the early Playstation and Xbox consoles, video game characters were able to do so much more, visually, graphically, and even with sound, than the earlier consoles allowed. In the 2000-2010 decade, many classic characters were made over to fit the new consoles, with new looks, sounds, adventures, and friends, but many new characters emerged.

It was the new characters, from new games and franchises that *Game Informer* considered for their article "Top 30 Characters that defined the Decade."

The characters in this article, selected by the *Game Informer* staff were recognized as the "most fully realized characters we've ever seen." [1] For the publication, *Game Informer* wrote up a description of each character, including artwork and the character's role in the overall story of their game. The thirty characters they chose were the result of the "explosion of creativity" that spawned from exciting consoles, upgraded graphics and capabilities of the newest gaming systems. The last decade was a time when the video games stopped being an amusement and turned into a true art form. Video game characters took on a life of their own, with lives that became more complex, three-dimensional and meaningful than their predecessors. [2]

Of the thirty characters listed in the article, twenty two are exclusively male, seven are exclusively female. Only one of the characters, Commander Shepard from the *Mass Effect* Series (2007-2012) can be either male or female. [1]

Shepard, as either male or female, is a special case, and will not be considered as "male" or "female" for the time being.

Gender breakdown of the top thirty

The list of male characters has a wide variety of character types. Sixteen of the Male characters are exclusively playable characters, PCs. Three of the male characters are exclusively presented as non-player characters. The three

---

[1] For a breakdown of the characters, their names, and their respective roles within their game roles, a quick reference chart has been compiled in Appendix A.

remaining male characters can be either PC or NPC, depending on the situation of the main player character within the game.

Because so many of the male characters on the lists are playable characters, they can be considered protagonists. Antagonists are primarily non-playable characters within video games. Of the six total male characters that are not player characters, three are antagonists. Only one of these three of the antagonist/non-playable characters can also be a PC.

None of the seven exclusively female characters are both PC and NPC. Five of these seven are fully non-playable, two are fully playable. Two of the seven female characters are fully robotic or android characters, compared to a single male robot.

The number one character on the list, Gla-DOS, is a non-humanoid antagonist female. Gla-DOS, short for Genetic Lifeform and Disk Operating System, premiered in 2007's *Portal*. She starts off as "little more than a benign advisor" to the protagonist, offering the player cake, assuring the player that "nothing is wrong" while trying to steer the playable character to their death and ultimately becomes *Portal*'s primary antagonist.[3]

Until the end scenario of the game, GLa-DOS is a voice-over; only in the end of the game does the player see her robotic, non-humanoid form. She is a disembodied voice until the player, a silent woman named Chell. In the end battle, the strategy to kill Gla-DOS is interesting. As she taunts the player, Gla-DOS drops round, almost egg-shaped devices, that she calls "reality cores" from her body. By destroying the cores, damage her.

A purely psychotherapeutic interpretation of this would show that this evil nasty passive-aggressive robot is killed by her symbolic babies. She doesn't actually die; her consciousness survives; she taunts the player with an eerie song, "I'm Still alive" as she dies.

Alyx Vance is the "human face on an otherwise abstract sci-fi story," and "the emotional center" to *Half Life 2* (2004). Alyx is not necessarily the girlfriend of the main character, her role is not to exist "solely for [a] romantic relationship with the male protagonist" but a romantic link is hinted upon. [4] The relationship, or that part of the relationship, is not important to the game, or the story of the game.

The *Uncharted* (2007-2012) series' Elena Fisher is a "fiercely intelligent reporter" who crosses paths with the protagonist Nathan Drake. Nathan Drake is much like Indiana Jones, Lara Croft, and a daredevil. Elena is his sidekick and love interest.[5] In the first two of the *Uncharted* games, the couple engages in a wildly flirtatious and dangerous relationship. Sometime between the second and third game, Drake and Fisher marry and separate, driven back together by the events of the third game.

"The Boss" in *Metal Gear Solid 3: Snake Eater* is a pivotal character in the *Metal Gear* mythology, ultimately acting as a rival and martyr.[6] She is a mentor, a mother-figure, an actual mother, and a rival.[7]

The final female NPC on the list, Bonnie MacFarlane is a feisty rancher woman. She teaches the player game play mechanics, tends to the protagonists wounds, and is a "real woman," who "displays a full range of emotions, some spoken, other subtly conveyed through body language and tone."[8] Bonnie is a rancher, she is the 'man of the house' with her father and brothers gone, and she provides the protagonist with a number of side quests and missions. Bonnie is not a love interest, the main player character of the game is a married man named John Marston. It is implied that Bonnie had feelings for John, but as John is a faithful husband, that type of relationship is never developed.

While all five of these female NPCs do not intentionally act in traditional female roles, by serving as caretakers, lovers, teachers, and mother-figures, female NPCs default to the traditional roles.

The two remaining exclusively female characters are playable characters.

KOS-MOS, the first of these two characters, is from the *Xenosaga* Series (2002-2006). She is an "unstoppable robotic war machine driven by cold logic" and extremely protective of her master/creator, Shion, the main protagonist of the game.

KOS-MOS is a robot with a mind for rational thought, and logic. She's strong, fast, and easily more powerful than the other player characters. Her role in the series is so complicated that understanding it "practically requires advanced degrees in philosophy and religion." Throughout three games of the *Xenosaga* series, KOS-MOS remains a complex mystery, only understood after the end of the story.[9]

The second female playable character, Jade (*Beyond Good and Evil*) has a driving goal to defend an orphanage and discover the truth behind political corruption. While Jade can, and does, use combat in the game, she is primarily a spy-type character- a photojournalist who sneaks into various classified locations to discover the truth. Jade is remembered for "her dedication to the people she loves and her unwillingness to turn away or back down in the face of danger."[10] Both KOS-MOS and Jade protect their loved ones, one through overt combative techniques and the other through stealthy actions. However, both Jade and KOS-MOS are care-takers and teachers.

Commander Shepard

The only character on the list that could be both male and female was Commander Shepard, the protagonist and primary playable character for the *Mass Effect* series. Shepard is not unique in the modern video game. Shepard is the only character of the "30 Characters" list that can be either Male or Female, depending solely on the choice of the player.[11] The male model for Commander Shepard is the "iconic figurehead for [BioWare's] *Mass Effect* franchise."[12] As one of the thirty characters, *Game Informer* explains that Shepard is memorable because she or he "feels like a naturally progressing individual along any number of different story branches."[13]

Shepard is a special case, indeed. Within each game of the *Mass Effect* series, Shepard has the opportunity to make moral decisions that effect later areas within the game. A choice in part one can change character options in part two, and even more options in part three. Shepard has a variety of love interests—human or otherwise, male or female, heterosexual or homosexual. The player has the option to ignore sexuality and romance all together within the games or to have romances cross from one game to the next

.

All while saving the universe from creatures seeking to wipe out and destroy all organic life forms.

When the player can choose either gender

The discussion of Shepard brings to mind other games that allow a video gamer to make open decisions about their character's gender and sexuality.

BioWare, who produced the *Mass Effect* series and its protagonist Shepard, also made the *Dragon Age* series, and the Mass multiplayer online role-playing game (MMORPG) *Ultima Online*.

The first game in the *Dragon Age* series *Dragon Age Origins*, gives the player the choice to play a number of races, (Elf, Dwarf, Human) and job types (Warrior, Thief, Mage) of either gender. Romance options exist that are solely for female, solely for male, or bisexual options. The romance of the player character may even lead to the PC running the nation of Ferelden as King or Queen.

Dragon Age: Origins, the first game of the *Dragon Age* series, offered two bisexual companions (one male, one female), two heterosexual companions (one male, one female), an optional quest that gives players the option to participate in an orgy, and a brothel with unlimited options for sexual encounters.

Dragon Age II, explores the war-torn world of Thedas. Like Commander Shepard from *Mass Effect, Dragon Age II* offers a PC, Hawke, a "mythical and charismatic figure," that can be either female or male.[14] The player can manipulate and control gender, skin tone, and facial features of both Hawke and Shepard. Hawke is exclusively human, but can be mage, rouge, or warrior.

As the gamer controls Hawke, she can make decisions for the character that influence Thedas or the relationship with companion characters, which are non-player characters in the player's control. The player has the option to participate in romantic relationships with the companion characters. This option is not limited to heterosexual relationships or even to a single race.[15]

Dragon Age II offers five companion relationship options (three Male, two female companions) and a number of "other encounters;" all but one of the companion relationships in *Dragon Age II* are available as romantic options for either Male or Female PCs.[16] All of the companions are bisexual, except for one of the males.

Not all players of *Dragon Age II* were happy with the romantic options available in the new game. "Bastal," who identifies himself as a "straight male gamer" did not enjoy the romantic options of the BioWare game. Bastal explains:

> In every previous BioWare game, I always felt that almost every companion in the game was designed for the male gamer in mind. Every female love interest was always written as a male friend type support character. In Dragon Age 2, I felt like most of the companions were designed to appeal to other groups foremost . . . It makes things very awkward when your male companions keep making passes at you.[17]

Bastal continues by expressing a belief that BioWare should have included a "no Homosexuality" option for the game. He complains that the two "female romance companions" were "'exotic' choices" and "weren't even . . . an option most males will like . . . [BioWare] had the resources to add another romance option, but instead chose to implement a gay romance with Anders."[18] Isabella, a human pirate, is not exotic; Merrill, the elf mage, might be considered exotic, based on her racial differences.

Bastal's argument centers on the idea that the "Straight Male Gamer" is the primary demographic for videogames. His guess was that 80% of RPG fans were males, and that less than 5% of RPG fans are homosexual. Women are increasingly playing video games, and online games. One study found that in 2001, female gamers were surpassing males as online players.[19] Hilde G. Corneliussen explained that women, especially women over 40, have become a large market for computer games. Conreliussen quoted Entertainment Software Association (ESA) statistics, "Women age 18 or older represent a greater portion of the game-playing population (30%) than boys age 17 or younger."[20]

Though these two studies refer to online games, they show that the community of video gamers is not heterogeneous; it is neither exclusively male nor young.

Take just a moment and digest that bit of information.

Grown-up women play more video games than teenage boys.

There are the obvious factors that adult women usually make more money than teenagers, but also, adult women are not blocked by the game maturity ratings when they attempt to purchase or rent video games. A sixteen year old boy attempting to purchase *Mass Effect, Dragon Age, Half Life*, or *Call of Duty* should be prevented from buying the game because of legal restrictions surrounding the sale of mature-rated games to minors. Adult women, those 18 and up, do not have that restriction.

It is highly short-sighted to assume that only young males play video games.

David Gaider, the lead writer of the *Dragon Age* series, replied to Bastal's complaints, "The romances in the game are not for the 'straight male gamer.' They're for everyone. We have a lot of fans, many of whom are neither straight nor male, and they deserve no less attention."[21]

To Bastal's charge that the designers should have included one heterosexual romance option for the male characters, Gaider explained, "The truth is that making a romance available for both genders is far less costly than creating an entirely new one." And that the only thing Gaider would change is to remove companion-initiation of a relationship. [22]

The *Fable* series, produced by Lionhead Studios, has a different method of approaching gender. In all three games, the PC, called the Hero, embarks on a quest to save the nation of Albion. In the first *Fable* (2004), the Hero was a male character, who could dress in women's clothing and have sexual relationships with male or female NPCs, and even have multiple marriages throughout the game world. In *Fable II* (2008), the Hero could be either male or female, and have relationships or marriages with either male or female NPCs. Another addition to *Fable II* included reproduction; the Hero could have children with a spouse or adopt children. *Fable III* (2010) continued with the *Fable II* approach to sexuality. *Fable III* female Heroes can marry and have children, adopt, and eventually, rule the world. In both games, the Hero parent leaves children in the care of the other parent. Regardless of the gender of the Hero. A female Hero's babies are raised by her Male (or female) spouse. The female Hero of *Fable* is not bound or constrained by gender roles.

Throughout the three games, the appearance of the Hero is shaped by the actions chosen by the player: evil actions cause the Hero to look menacing, Heroes who use a lot of physical skills "bulk up," magic-using PCs grow mystical auras. Female Heroes in *Fable II* build strong upper body muscles, in the same way that the male Heroes in the game do. Online discussions of *Fable II*'s female Hero often discussed "trading tips on how to keep their female heroes demure- even if the tradeoff was a drastic reduction in brute strength."[23] The Hero can be scarred, attractive, thin, and bulky, all depending on how the player controls the Hero's actions. Essentially, building physical strength in *Fable II* meant that the female Hero ceased to look feminine.

Fable II and *Fable III* illustrate fascinating aspects of the argument of female-body imagery in video games. The design of a female playable character is no more difficult than the creation of a male playable character, but including both as options requires "double the render work, motion capturing, and voice acting" and the designers must be careful to ensure "dialogue and ambient chatter . . . avoid gender-specific references." Inclusion of a male and female PC "doubles the cost of the whole game in many respects."[24] Jennifer Wildes, art director at Gearbox software, explains:

> It turns out that women are shaped differently, they move differently, and they sound different. It's kind of a pain. In the end, though, if these aspects aren't considered, you end up with a character that is less than you deserve, or have made tradeoffs in the development process that you may regret.[25]

Even if the female and male PCs make similar ranges of motions, game designers striving for realism in their computer-model characters must consider these aspects while constructing the games.

Designing a female protagonist could provide the game designer with anxiety. The ultimate female protagonist must:

> [be] relatable so that both male and female players want to play as them. But for a female character, they have to be attractive (but not sl*tty *sic*), kick butt (but not too butch), and be smart (but not too nerdy).[26]

The designer must worry about fan reactions to their female characters. Male characters rarely get called "too slutty" or "too masculine."

Many mass multiplayer online role-playing games (MMORPGs) often have different types of character selection processes. Players not only choose gender of the character, but race. Race in role-playing games and MMORPGs like *World of Warcraft* or *Everquest* often offer racial varieties similar to those found in fantasy novels: humans, elves, dwarves, orcs, each with attributes, advantages, and disadvantages for the selection. Among the different races, the characters are often further customizable, to fit the desires of the player. One MMORPG player selected her character race because the "cute Wood elf" was beautiful, and she "wanted to be her."[27] Another MMORPG player explained what she wanted in her choice of avatars:

> I certainly want the ability to play a woman, and I want to be able to decide what she looks like as much as possible. I want my characters to be beautiful, but not necessarily brazen, and I certainly don't want to be

forced to display even virtual buttocks to the world to the howls of laughter from my fellow players.[28]

The "virtual buttocks" or "chain mail bikini" stereotype is that of the scantily clad female hero, who dresses for male's enjoyment.

Female Bodies in Video Games: Lara Croft the Icon.

There are many complaints to the construction of the female body in video games. Game females, like comic book heroines, Barbie dolls and women on magazine covers, are blamed for encouraging poor body imagery in young girls and women. A study of female characters found that video game females, on average, had larger heads, smaller chests, smaller waists, and smaller hips than the Civilian American and European Surface Anthropometry Resource (CAESAR) study model of "average" American female proportions.[29] In a comparison of realism, the more realistic characters "conformed more to the thin-ideal than did the less realistic characters" and were "significantly smaller" than the CAESAR sample.[30] If the average female game character were real, she would be "5'4' tall, with a 29" bust, 22" waist, and 31" hips."[31] Thus, the average female video game character fits a thin-body ideal type.

To many, the "ultimate" female video game character is Lara Croft, from the *Tomb Raider* series. Sometimes called a "female equivalent of an Indiana Jones," Lara Croft is a popular image in the video game world.[32] Although she is a video game character, Lara Croft is often treated like a real person; *Entertainment Weekly* magazine once listed Lara as "one of the 100 most creative people in entertainment."[33] Throughout several video games and two feature films, Lara has become the iconic video game female. She does not sit in a palace waiting to be rescued; she explores, and is "idolized as an independent adventurous woman who gets what she wants—not through sex, but through her prowess."[34] The spunky, adventurous side of Lara is accompanied with Lara's sexual image. Lara Croft "exudes feminine masculinity, and . .

. rather than challenging masculine dominance, feeds it and makes [it] acceptable through feminine curves, seductive lips, and over-sized eyes."[35]

The earliest models of Lara Croft (see figure 1) "resemble[e] a 'pin-up' with conspicuously thin waist and hips and large breasts."[36] Croft is the male fantasy, "the empty shell to be filled by male desire."[37] To sell the image of Croft, Core Design Ltd., the originators of the *Tomb Raider* franchise, would hire real look-alike models to appear at trade shows; these Lara Croft models worked hard to maintain the look of Lara.[38] When one male fan travelled by bicycle over a long distance to meet "Lara Croft," one model, Lucy Clarkson, obliged the fan with a date; the fan did not see this as a date with Lucy, but a date with Lara.[39]

Maja Mikula explains that much of the discourse on gender and video gaming takes a gendered approach; women "identify" with the characters they play, while men "control" the character.[40] Lara Croft's dual imagery is a good example of this identity/control discourse. An early player of *Tomb Raider* described himself as "more cautious and protective" of Lara than other game characters. Male players expressed dissatisfaction at the brief introduction of a male character in a later Tomb Raider game because *Tomb Raider* was about "controlling a female character as feisty and attractive as Lara."[41] Female players often feel empowered by Lara, and enjoy *being* Lara in game play.[42]

The next incarnation of Lara Croft, *Tomb Raider* (2011), is going to be a reboot of the franchise. Lara Croft in *Tomb Raider* will be young and inexperienced.[43] Lara Croft of 2011 has been redesigned, remodeled. Brian Horton, senior art director at Crystal Dynamics, the new home of *Tomb Raider,* explained, "What we chose to do very early on with Lara was not to start with the surface qualities and instead really work on who she was as a character."[44] The designers wanted her to be more human, more empathetic, and more relatable; Lara's "Teflon coating" was her biggest downfall.[45] To help this, the new Lara has a "softer, rounder face."[46] Instead of Lara's traditional appearance (large breasts, thin waist), Lara has smaller breasts, she is "more believable."[47] While Lara still falls under the "thin ideal," she no longer has exaggerated breasts (fig. 2). While the new Lara Croft should downplay Croft as a sexual icon, not everyone believes the new Lara will be a good thing. One female player, in writing to *Game Informer* complained, "I won a year's supply of martinis for my Lara Croft impression last Halloween. How am I supposed to emulate the small-chested, wider-hipped rendition?"[48]

There are many disagreements as to Croft's place in society. To some, she embodies the strong, independent woman. Croft is "the sole survivor of a plane crash, who used her wilderness skills to stay alive for two weeks—as well as being a trained rock climber, expert shooter, motorcyclist, and world famous archaeologist."[49] To others, she is the sex kitten, a near-pornographic sex symbol that exists as part of male fantasy. Lara Croft is "everything that is bad . . . and everything that is good" of images of women in culture.[50] She is simultaneously a sex symbol and a role model.

Interacting with Others

Online game playing consists of any video-game where players interact online with other players of the same game. The most common form of online play comes in the Mass Multiplayer Online Role Playing Games (MMORPGs) like *World of Warcraft* or in online virtual worlds like *Second Life*. Other types of online play link players of First-person shooter (FPS) games with one another or link players of music game players, like the *Guitar Hero* or *Rock Band* series. Online game play can be competitive, between individual players, cooperative, or both and generally offer the chance for the player to interact with players outside of their home.

When females play, and succeed, in first-person shooter games, it can result in extreme negative reaction from male players. When talking about her experience playing *Call of Duty: Modern Warfare* (2007) one female player explained, "As soon as the guys figure out I am a girl it starts. Insults, name calling, and general loud mouthing, and it gets worse when I have more kills than anyone in the game."[51] Perhaps the threatening language and negativity is not entirely due to gender. The *Game Informer* editor responds, "regardless of sex . . . you can always expect to have a boatload of bigotry and vulgarities hurled at you," especially if the player "finish[es] at the top of the leader boards."[52] The hyper-masculine environment of FPS games leads to the trash-talking, vulgar language and competitive nature. When a male player is defeated, he feels threatened; when he is defeated by "a girl," he feels humiliated.

A high number of players of online games do so for the chance to work cooperatively with other players. Many players of MMORPGs play online when their local friends or romantic partners are available to play. [53] Studies of game play suggest that excessive play of MMORPGs can ruin real-life relationships and friendships.[54] At least one-quarter MMORPG players play with family members and real-life friends; female players were far more likely to socialize with friends and family from outside of MMORPGS require social interaction in order to accomplish missions, which help players foster relationships with the other online players. Less than half of MMORPG players believed their friends online compared with real-life friendships.[55] One study found that three-quarters of all MMORPG players form friendships within games; Males typically formed *more* online relationships than females while females were more likely to form "emotionally stronger friendships, with the ability to discuss sensitive issues" than male players.[56]

Because females form stronger relationships with their online friends, some might assume that female players might prefer online game play and select character types that encourage online cooperation. Two common character types in the MMORPG are the Warrior, which includes soldiers, barbarians, knights, and the Healer, which includes enchanters, clerics, shamans, and druids.[57] Healer types often encourage cooperative play, requiring the player to work along with a group of fellow players while warriors are combat-intensive. Michele Companion and Roger Sambrook found that women often prefer to play solo-game experiences and prefer Healer character types because of an aversion to violence instead of the desire to help their companions.[58]

The MMORPG offers more than the chance for the player to socialize online. It offers players a chance to explore and construct identities unique for the world. The player can explore identities regardless of their offline personality. Women can explore the world of an online community while "practic[ing] more assertive behavior" and "can travel [the online world] knowing they are no more threatened by the creatures of the world than their male counterparts are."[59] Women can play violently to "express aggression in a safe context."[60] The player can also explore gender identity.

Zaheer Hussain and Mark Griffiths found that 57% of MMORPG gamers engage in gender-swapping at some point in their online game-playing experiences.[61] Different reasons for online gender swapping were given by the players. On player stated, "It enables me to play around with aspects of my character that are not normally easy to experiment with in real life." One female player stated, "I made my male character because I was tired of creepy guys hitting on my female characters." Other players cited better treatment by fellow players and lower costs for inter-player exchanges as reasons for playing cross-gender.[62] Some players play cross-gender to 'look at something pretty.'[63] Another MMORPG player explained:

> Sometimes I make a male character and don't let anyone know I'm a female in real life. It's interesting how different people treat you when they think you are male. Kind of like a window into their strange man universe.[64]

Cross-gender play in online video games allows men and women explore at "playing" the other gender or allow them opportunities otherwise unavailable.

Second Life allows the "residents" to interact with others world wide, instead of playing to meet objectives, people in *Second Life* socialize and interact with one another. Unlike

World of Warcraft or other MMORPGs, *Second Life* does not have clearly defined objective; the creators of *Second Life* encourage participants to manipulate the world.[65] Modifications to *Second Life* include everything from buildings, vehicles, and clothing to genitals.[66]

Sex is not the primary focus or purpose of *Second Life*. However, when an avatar is suspected of being a cross-gendered avatar, the assumption is that it is always for a sexual motive. Like play within *World of Warcraft*, *Second Life* players explore the world, interact with one another, and experiment in assertiveness. *Second Life* can provide an opportunity to interact with others, and explore the world.

Gender-swapping in *Second Life* can be problematic. Unlike *World of Warcraft*, where players are participating in missions together, *Second Life* players are socializing and communicating with one another. Male players flirting with female avatars might feel very threatened by the possibility of a male player "on the other side." A player using a cross-gender avatar is not necessarily using the avatar as a means to meet sexual partners or participate in sexual activity. The avatar might be a chance for the player to explore living as the other gender. Transgender players of *Second Life* may use the world of *Second Life* as a chance to live without fear of persecution.

Avatars in *Second Life* with genitals have the option to participate in a range of sexual activities, either active or passive, by activating "pose balls;" pose balls include "hand jobs," "Blowjobs" and rape.[67] For an avatar to participate in any animation, the player must select the pose ball for the given action. Thus, victim avatars in rape scenes must select the rape pose ball. The "rape ball" presents a "disturbing" and "problematic" thought; either the female player is complicit in a rape scene *or* a male player has created a female avatar "with the purpose of having her submit to sexual violation and humiliation."[68] Prostitution also occurs in *Second Life*. The world of *Second Life* uses Linden Dollars, exchangeable for real US currency, which can be used to pay for everything, including sexual services.

Because the avatar *might* be of a different gender than the player, some men in *Second Life* might want to seek verification of the women they "patronize" as escorts; voice-software was created to certify females as "GVF" (gender-verified female).[69] Transgender players protested the software, exclaiming that the voice-verification was "a threat to their existence in [*Second Life*]" because "being forced to use a voice in the virtual world . . . against my will . . . feels like the ultimate blow."[70] If the Transgender player uses *Second Life* as a chance to live in their true gender without retribution or mockery, gender-verification is a true threat to the transgendered player's chance to experiment with gender identity.

As Seen on the Silver Screen

The film *Gamer* (2009) portrays a science fiction future where technology of video games has progressed significantly beyond the standards of today. Unlike any of the games discussed in this research, the characters in *Gamer* are living humans, controlled by another human player. Gender of the avatars in *Gamer* drastically affects the way the players use their avatars and the way those outside the game treat them.

In *Gamer*, player-controlled avatars are not digital characters but living humans, altered with technology to allow players to control their actions. Players pay to live, or die, as other people in either game. In *Gamer*, the two most popular games are *Society* and *Slayers*. The game *Slayers* is a deadly and dangerous third-person shooter game; the avatar is completely visible on screen and game play consists of shooting. The other game, *Society*, is a simulation game similar to *Second Life* or *The Sims*, where the avatar socializes with other avatars.

Slayers fight in rigid combative situations, much like the games *Half Life*, *Call of Duty*, *Gears of War* and *Halo*. Avatar characters in *Slayers* are death-row inmates who volunteer for the game; if they survive 30 missions, they are released from their sentence. The avatars in *Slayers* volunteer for the role in hopes of gaining release. "Gener-icons," described as a male or female prisoner who "couldn't hack it as a Slayer" but deserve the chance at freedom, gain release after surviving a single mission. It is unclear if the gener-icons are death row inmates. No Slayer or gener-icon has ever survived the game. The primary Slayer character in the game, "Kable/John Tillman," portrayed by Gerard Butler, is the first Avatar to come close to completing the 30 mission goal.

While on the set of *Society*, avatars react as their players react. While "on set" players control *Society* avatars; the way an avatar dresses, the words they say, the placement of their bodies, are all in control of the player instead of the body of the actor. Actions made by avatars in *Gamer* are do not affect the player at home; the player can engage in wild sex, combat situations, and shoot outs without injury or illness. As in *Second Life,* sexual encounters in *Society* could be with any other avatar, regardless of gender of the avatar or the player of the avatar.

Amber Valetta portrays "Angie Tillman/Nika" Kable's wife and a *Society* avatar controlled by the overweight male Gorge. There are no gender-verifications of the avatars for *Society;* when *Gorge* speaks, it is with Nika's voice. Gorge uses Nika in *Society* to gratify his sexual desires through controlling her in (sometimes violent) sexual encounters with strangers. "Nika" consumes drinks worm-infested liquor and suffers sexual and physical abuses that would otherwise not be willful experiences of Angie Tillman. When confronting an avatar named "Rick Rape," Angie's leg jerks nervously, while Nika remains calm while talking. Gorge allows Nika's assaults and attacks. Angie *might* be reacting to a person who has assaulted her in the past. Gorge, in control, forces Nika to communicate, talk, and flirt with a former assailant.

Gender roles in *Gamer* are rigid. While there are many female *Society* avatars, there are few female *Slayers. Slayers* avatars are referred to as men or women, but most of the *Slayers* are male. "Kable" meets one female *Slayer,* Sondra, and witnesses a truck run over a veiled woman within the game. The disparity between male and female avatars in *Slayers* is not explained, but could be because of the scarcity of female death-row inmates. Another reason could be that

Slayers serves as a live-action version of games like *Halo, Army of Two,* and the *Call of Duty* series; few females serve in combative roles within these games because they seek to emulate current standards of military combat, where few women serve in combative positions.[71]

Nika/Angie has legal difficulties due to her role in *Society.* Her husband, *Slayers* avatar Kable/John is a hero because of his outstanding win record. Kable's player receives a number of financial bids, including one for 50, then 100 million Euros, for his avatar. Kable, who will be the first *Slayers* avatar to survive 30 matches, could gain great financial advantages after his release from the game. Despite the 'criminal' past of John Tillman, he is in a potentially advantageous situation because he is a war hero from an invented war. Angie is a law-abiding citizen who viewed with disgust, little more than a prostitute, because of her job in *Society.* Angie risks losing custody of her daughter because of her husband John's death-row conviction and her disreputable career.

Conclusions

In a video game world, gender is a complex construction. Female characters in video games often fall into stereotypical or traditional roles. Designing a female character is no more difficult than designing a male one, but inclusion of both as playable characters requires twice the work. Designers risk sharp criticism for fans for creating "unrealistic" women. Although few women appeared in the top 30 characters of the last decade, female characters in video games are shifting from the "damsel in distress" and sex kitten to the heroine in control. Some videogame companies, like BioWare and Lionhead Studios, work to improve the depiction of female and homosexual game characters. Cross-gendered play in video games is common. Online cross-gendered players, when discovered, can meet with derision and disrespect by those who feel 'betrayed' by the player's 'act.'

Appendix A: *The Thirty Characters*

Name	Game	20	Gender	NPC	PC	Robot?
GLaDOS	**Portal**	**7**	**F**	**x/Antagonist**		**X**
John Marston	*Red Dead Redemption*	10	M		X	
Nathan Drake	*Uncharted Series*	7	M		X	
Master Chief	*Halo Series*	1	M		X	
Niko Bellic	*Grand Theft Auto IV*	8	M		X	
Alyx Vance	***Half Life 2***	**4**	**F**	**X/Lover?**		
Kratos	*God Of War Series*	5	M		x	
Andrew Ryan	*Bioshock*	7	M	x/antagonist		
Loghain mac tir	*Dragon Age: Origins*	9	M	x/antagonist	X	
Ezio Auditore da Firenze	*Assassin's Creed Series*	9	M		X	
Ethan Mars	*Heavy Rain*	10	M		X	
Commander	***Mass***	**7**	**m/f**		**x**	

Shepard	*Effect Series*					
Jimmy Hopkins	*Bully*	6	M		X	
Captain John Price	*Call of Duty Series*	7	M	X	x	
HK-47	*Star Wars: Knights of the Old Republic series*	3	M		x	X
Elena Fisher	*Uncharted Series*	7	F	**X/Lover**		
Illusive Man	*Mass Effect Series*	8	M	x/antagonist		
Tommy Vercetti	*Grand Theft Auto: Vice City*	2	M		X	
The Boss	*Metal Gear Series*	4	F	**X/Mother figure/Rival**		
Tim	*Braid*	8	M		X	
Auron	*Final Fantasy X, X-2*	1	M		X	
Razputin "Raz" Aquato	*Psychonauts*	5	M		x	
Kaim Argonar	*Lost Odyssey*	7	M		x	

Jade	*Beyond Good and Evil*	3	F		X	
KOS-MOS	*Xenosaga Series*	3	F		X	X
Professor Layton	*Professor Layton Series*	7	M		x	
Phoenix Wright	*Ace Attorney Series*	1	M		x	
Wander	*Shadow of the Colossus*	5	M		X	
Bonnie MacFarlane	*Red Dead Redemption*	10	F	X/ally		
King of all Cosmos	*Katamari*	4	M	X/mentor		

Taken from "The 30 Characters Who Defined a Decade" *Game Informer* December 2010, p 46-69. *Chart constructed by Amanda Oviatt for purpose of this research project.* Characters are listed in order as presented in the original article.

Bolded characters are Female.

Appendix B: Works Cited

Magazine Articles

    Game Informer Editor. "Reply to Jessica from Lyndhurst." *Game, Informer* October, 2010.

    Game Informer Staff. "The 30 Characters Who Defined a Decade." *Game Informer,* December, 2010.

    Jessica, from Lyndhurst, NJ. "Letter to the Editor." *Game Informer,* October, 2010.

    Juba, Joe *"Dragon Age II." Game Informer,* August, 2010.

    Marie, Megan. "The Gender Gap." *Game Informer.com,* March 25, 2010. (accessed April 4, 2011). This article was originally published in *Game Informer* March, 2010.

    Marie, Megan. "Tomb Raider," *Game Informer,* January 2011.

    Valerie from Tampa, Fl. "Letter to the Editor." *Game Informer,* March, 2011.

Game Informer is a magazine published by *GameStop,* and is used to preview, review, and inform the general public about upcoming and new release video game titles. Because I seek to discover gender in current video games, I have chosen to use some articles from the last year's editions of *Game Informer.*

Online Resources

Bastal. "Bioware Neglected Their Main Demographic: The Straight Male Gamer." *BioWare Social Network,* http://social.bioware.com/forum/1/topic/304/index /6661775&lf=8 (accessed April 4, 2011). Used to show a single fan's reaction to sexuality in Bioware's *Dragon Age II.*

Gaider, David. "BioWare response to Bastal's forum posting." *BioWare Social Network,* http://social.bioware.com/forum/1/topic/304/index /6661775&lf=8 (accessed April 5, 2011). David Gaider is one of the lead writers for the *Dragon Age* series.

JoeHawke, editor. "Romance *(Dragon Age II)."* *Dragon Age Wiki.* http://dragonage.wikia.com/wiki/Romance_(Dragon _Age_II) (accessed April 4, 2011). This web posting is used to assist the writer in explanation of Romance in Dragon Age II.

Metal Gear Wiki, "The Boss." http://metalgear.wikia.com/wiki/The_Boss (accessed April 4, 2011). This web posting is used to determine the purpose of the Boss in Metal Gear Solid.

Books

Corneliussen, Hilde, *"World of Warcraft* as a Playground for Feminism," in *Digital Culture, Play, and Identity: A Critical Anthology of World of Warcraft Research*, edited by Hilde Corneliussen and Jill Walker Reitberg, 72-95. Cambridge, MA: MIT Press, 2008. This book offers an interesting and scholarly approach to the *World of Warcraft* and Mass Multiplayer Online Role Playing Games.

Taylor, T.L. "Where the Women Are." In *Play Between Worlds: Exploring Online Game Culture*, 93-124. Cambridge, Ma: MIT Press, 2008. This book is an examination of online games and the culture surrounding online gaming.

Scholarly Articles

Brookey, Robert Alan & Kristopher L. Cannon, "Sex Lives in *Second Life*," *Critical Studies in Media Communication* 26 no 2 (June, 2009): 145-164.

Cole, Helena, and Mark Griffiths. "Social Interactions in Massively Multiplayer Online Role-Playing Gamers." *CyberPsychology & Behavior* 10 no 4, (2007): 575-583.

Companion, Michele and Roger Sambrook. "The Influence of Sex on Character Attribute Preferences." *CyberPsychology & Behavior* 11 no 6 (2008): 673-674.

Hussain, Zaheer, and Mark D. Griffiths, "Gender Swapping and Socializing in Cyberspace: An Exploratory Study." *CyberPsychology & Behavior* 11 no 1 (2008):47-53.

------., "The Attitudes, Feelings, and Experiences of Online Gamers: A Qualitative Analysis," *CyberPsychology &Behavior* 12 no 6, (2009): 747-753.

Lancaster, Kurt. "Lara Croft: The Ultimate Young Adventure Girl or the Unending Media Desire for Models, Sex, and Fantasy?" *Paj: A Journal of Performance and Art* 26 no 3 (2004): 87-97.

Martins, Nicole, Dmitri C. Williams, Kristen Harrison, and Rabindra A. Ratan. "A Content Analysis of Female Body Imagery in Video Games." *Sex Roles* 61 (2009): 824-836.

Mikula, Maja. "Gender and Videogames: The Political Valency of Lara Croft," *Continuum: Journal of Media & Cultural Studies,* 17 no 1 (2003): 79-87.

Games Referenced
Arnold, Vicky and Toby Gard. *Tomb Raider, featuring Lara Croft.* Disk Based-Game. Great Britain, Core Design, 1996.

BioWare, *Dragon Age: Origins.* Disk-Based Game. Edmonton, Alberta, Canada, 2009.

------. *Dragon Age II.* Disk-Based Game. Edmonton, Alberta, Canada, 2010.

Gard, Toby, Paul Douglas, Martin Iveson, and Nathan McCree. *Tomb Raider.* Disc-Based Game. San Francisco, Ca: Crystal Dynamics, 2011.

Molyneux, Peter. *Fable*. Disc-Based Game. Guildford, Surrey, UK: Lionhead Studios, 2004.

------. *Fable II*. Disc-Based Game. Guildford, Surrey, UK: Lionhead Studios, 2008.

------. *Fable III*. Disc-Based Game. Guildford, Surrey, UK: Lionhead Studios, 2010.

Nintendo Team Ninja. *Metroid*. Cartridge-based game. Japan, 1986.

Pardo, Rob, Jeff Kaplan, Tom Chilton, *World of Warcraft*. Online. Irvine, Ca: Blizzard Entertainment, 2004-2011.

Rosedale, Philip. *Second Life*. Online. San Francisco, Ca: Linden Labs. 1999-2011. http://secondlife.com/

Film
Butler, Gerard, Amber Valletta, and Michael C. Hall. *Gamer*. Netflix Streaming. Directed by Mark Neveldine and Brian Taylor. Albuquerque, NM: Lionsgate, 2009.

[1] Game Informer Staff, "The 30 Characters Who Defined a Decade," *Game Informer.* December 2010, 47.
[2] Ibid., 46.
[3] *Game Informer* Staff, 48.
[4] Ibid., 52.
[5] Ibid., 60.
[6] Ibid., 62.
[7] Metal Gear Wiki, "The Boss," http://metalgear.wikia.com/wiki/The_Boss (accesseed April 4, 2011).
[8] *Game Informer* Staff, 68.
[9] Ibid., 66.
[10] Ibid., 65.
[11] Ibid., 57.
[12] Megan Marie, "The Gender Gap" *Game Informer.com*, March 25, 2010, http://www.gameinformer.com/b/features/archive/2010/03/25/the-gender-gap.aspx?PostPageIndex=2 (accessed on on April 4, 2011.)
[13] *Game Informer* Staff, 57.
[14] Joe Juba, "*Dragon Age II,*" *Game Informer* August, 2010, 51.
[15] For the purpose of the *Dragon Age* series, race entails "human, elf, or dwarf" backgrounds.
[16] JoeHawke, editor "Romance (*Dragon Age II)*" *Dragon Age Wiki,* http://dragonage.wikia.com/wiki/Romance_(Dragon_Age_II) (accessed April 4, 2011).
[17] Bastal, "Bioware Neglected Their Main Demographic: The Straight Male Gamer," *BioWare Social Network* http://social.bioware.com/forum/1/topic/304/index/6661775&lf=8 (accessed April 4, 2011).
[18] Ibid.
[19] T.L. Taylor, "Where the Women Are," In *Play Between Worlds: Exploring Online Game Culture,* (Cambridge, Ma: MIT Press, 2008), 93.
[20] Hilde Corneliussen, "*World of Warcraft* as a Playground for Feminism," In *Digital Culture, Play, and Identity: A Critical Anthology of World of Warcraft Research,* edited by Hilde Corneliussen and Jill Walker Reitberg (Cambridge, MA: MIT Press, 2008), 75.
[21] David Gaider, "BioWare response to Bastal's forum posting," on *BioWare Social Network* http://social.bioware.com/forum/1/topic/304/index/6661775&lf=8 (accessed April 5, 2011).
[22] Ibid.
[23] Marie, "Gender Gap."
[24] Ibid,
[25] Ibid.
[26] Ibid.

[27] Taylor, 111.

[28] Ibid/,. 111.

[29] Nicole Martins, Dmitri C. Williams, Kristen Harrison, and Rabindra A. Ratan, "A Content Analysis of Female Body Imagery in Video Games," *Sex Roles* 61 (2009): 829.

[30] Ibid, 829-30.

[31] Ibid., 831.

[32] Kurt Lancaster, "Lara Croft: The Ultimate Young Adventure Girl or the Unending Media Desire for Models, Sex, and Fantasy?" *Paj: A Journal of Performance and Art* 26 no 3 (2004): 87.

[33] Lancaster , 87.

[34] Ibid., 88.

[35] Ibid., 88.

[36] Martins et al, 826.

[37] Lancaster, 88.

[38] Ibid., 90-1.

[39] Ibid., 92. She later received fan mail as "Lara" from the fan.

[40] Maja Mikula, "Gender and Videogames: The Political Valency of Lara Croft," *Continuum: Journal of Media & Cultural Studies,* 17 no 1 (2003): 81.

[41] Ibid.

[42] Ibid.

[43] Megan Marie, "Tomb Raider," *Game Informer,* January 2011, 42.

[44] Ibid., 45.

[45] Ibid., 41.

[46] Ibid., 45.

[47] Ibid.

[48] Valerie from Tampa, Fl, "Letter to the Editor" *Game Informer March,* 2011, 6. The editors replied "something tells us the judges of your costume contest probably won't mind if your costume next year doesn't accurately reflect Lara's new look."

[49] Mikula, 79.

[50] Ibid., 79-80.

[51] Jessica, from Lyndhurst, NJ, "Letter to the Editor" *Game Informer* October, 2010, 13.

[52] *Game Informer* Editor, "Reply to Jessica from Lyndhurst," *Game Informer* October, 2010, 13.

[53] Zaheer Hussain and Mark Griffiths, "The Attitudes, Feelings, and Experiences of Online Gamers: A Qualitative Analysis," *CyberPsychology &Behavior* 12 no 6, (2009): 749.

[54] Ibid., 750.

[55] Helena Cole and Mark Griffiths, "Social Interactions in Massively Multiplayer Online Role-Playing Gamers," *CyberPsychology & Behavior* 10 no 4, (2007): 579.

[56] Ibid., 581-82.

[57] Michele Companion and Roger Sambrook, "The Influence of Sex on Character Attribute Preferences," *CyberPsychology & Behavior* 11 no 6 (2008): 673.

[58] Ibid., 674.

[59] Taylor, 97.

[60] Ibid., 108.

[61]Zaheer Hussain and Mark D. Griffiths, "Gender Swapping and Socializing in Cyberspace: An Exploratory Study," *CyberPsychology & Behavior* 11 no 1 (2008): 50.

[62] Ibid.

[63] Two of my male friends prefer to use female avatars in all of their video games. They both give the reason, "Because I prefer to look at a girl's ass than a guy's while I'm roaming across the world."

[64] Ibid..

[65] Robert Alan Brookey & Kristopher L. Cannon, "Sex Lives in *Second Life*," *Critical Studies in Media Communication* 26 no 2 (June, 2009): 145.

[66] Ibid., 152.

[67] Ibid., 153.

[68] Ibid., 153.

[69] Ibid., 157

[70] Ibi., 158.

[71] Marie, "Gender Gap."

15508839R00027

Printed in Poland
by Amazon Fulfillment
Poland Sp. z o.o., Wrocław